The Jewish Americans

MARISSA LINGEN

WE CAME TO AMERICA

MASON CREST PUBLISHERS • PHILADELPHIA

Two Orthodox Jewish boys walk down a street in their Brooklyn neighborhood. Today, nearly half of the world's Jews live in the United States.

The Jewish Americans

MARISSA LINGEN

WE CAME TO AMERICA

MASON CREST PUBLISHERS • PHILADELPHIA

Mason Crest Publishers
370 Reed Road
Broomall PA 19008
www.masoncrest.com

First printing

1 3 5 7 9 8 6 4 2

Library of Congress Cataloging-in-Publication Data
on file at the Library of Congress

ISBN 1-59084-109-3

Table of Contents

WE CAME TO AMERICA

America's Ethnic Heritage

Barry Moreno, librarian
Statue of Liberty/
Ellis Island National Monument

Ethnic diversity is one of the most striking characteristics of the American identity. In the United States the Bureau of the Census officially recognizes 122 different ethnic groups. North America's population had grown by leaps and bounds, starting with the American Indian tribes and nations—the continent's original people—and increasing with the arrival of the European colonial migrants who came to these shores during the 16th and 17th centuries. Since then, millions of immigrants have come to America from every corner of the world.

But the passage of generations and the great distance of America from the "Old World"—Europe, Africa, and Asia—has in some cases separated immigrant peoples from their roots. The struggle to succeed in America made it easy to forget past traditions. Further, the American spirit of freedom, individualism, and equality gave Americans a perspective quite different from the view of life shared by residents of the Old World.

Immigrants of the 19th and 20th centuries recognized this at once. Many tried to "Americanize" themselves by tossing away their peasant clothes and dressing American-style even before reaching their new homes in the cities or the countryside of America. It was not so easy to become part of America's culture, however. For many immigrants, learning English was quite a hurdle. In fact, most older immigrants clung to the old ways, preferring to speak their native languages and follow their familiar customs and traditions. This was easy to do when ethnic neighborhoods abounded in large North American cities like New York, Montreal, Philadelphia, Chicago, Toronto, Boston, Cleveland, St. Louis, New Orleans and San Francisco. In rural areas, farm families—many of them Scandinavian, German, or Czech—established their own tightly knit communities. Thus foreign languages and dialects, religious beliefs, Old World customs, and certain class distinctions flourished.

The most striking changes occurred among the children of immigrants, whose hopes and dreams were different from those of their parents. They began breaking away from the Old World customs, perhaps as a reaction to the embarrassment of being labeled "foreigner." They badly wanted to be Americans, and assimilated more easily than their parents and grandparents. They learned to speak English without a foreign accent, to dress and act like other Americans. The assimilation of the children of immigrants was encouraged by social contact—games, schools, jobs, and military service—which further broke down the barriers between immigrant groups and hastened the process of Americanization. Along the way, many family traditions were lost or abandoned.

Today, the pride that Americans have in their ethnic roots is one of the abiding strengths of both the United States and Canada. It shows that the theory which called America a "melting pot" of the world's people was never really true. The thought that a single "American" would emerge from the combination of these peoples has never happened, for Americans have grown more reluctant than ever before to forget the struggles of their ethnic forefathers. The growth of cultural studies and genealogical research indicates that Americans are anxious not to entirely lose this identity, whether it is English, French, Chinese, African, Mexican, or some other group. There is an interest in tracing back the family line as far as records or memory will take them. In a sense, this has made Americans a divided people; proud to be Americans, but proud also of their ethnic roots.

As a result, many Americans have welcomed a new identity, that of the hyphenated American. This unique description has grown in usage over the years and continues to grow as more Americans recognize the importance of family heritage. In the end, this is an appreciation of America's great cultural heritage and its richness of its variety.

Two Jewish immigrants wait to be processed at Ellis Island, the immigration station in New York harbor. The skyline of New York City rises in the background of this late 19th-century photograph.

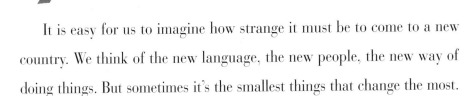

1 Coming to America

It is easy for us to imagine how strange it must be to come to a new country. We think of the new language, the new people, the new way of doing things. But sometimes it's the smallest things that change the most.

When Isaac Raboy came to New York with his family from Russia, he noticed everything about his new surroundings, but he was overjoyed with the only thing his parents could afford to buy him when they got off the ship. "I'd never had ice cream before. It was as new to me as America," he said. Buying ice cream for Isaac and his brother was his father's way of telling them that their new life in America would be different—and sweeter.

It was not hard to imagine a sweeter life than the one he had left. During the late 19th century, the Russian government openly **persecuted** its Jewish citizens, trying to get them to either leave the country or convert to Christianity. For many people—like the Raboys—this pressure worked.

The Raboys jammed themselves onto a boat bound for Germany with many other Russian Jewish families. From there, they could find transportation to the New World: a **steerage** passage. They were packed into the hold of a small ship with dozens of other passengers, many of whom became seasick during the voyage across the Atlantic Ocean. Getting off the ship at Ellis Island felt like heaven to Isaac, and the ice cream was the best part of his strange day arriving in America.

The Raboys made their way through the streets of New York to the Lower East Side, where many Jewish families lived. Even the people who were supposed to be familiar, his fellow Jews, looked strange to young Isaac. "Across Delancey Street, we passed young Jewish men and women. The girls had painted cheeks and greased netted hair with hidden pins....The males with stiff hats tipped over their foreheads and their plastered locks, gave off an aroma of vulgar, youthful *virility*. Who else was in the street? Elderly Jews and Jewesses, their mouths filled with gold; Jews hawking their wares from pushcarts filled with all that's exotic—I soon decided that here Jews live in the streets."

Back in the *shtetl*, his Jewish *ghetto* village in Russia, Isaac had seen Jews dressed simply and traditionally. No one could afford to wear makeup and cologne or even go to the dentist. In fact, there usually was no dentist. However, the young Jews Isaac saw on the streets of New York had lived in America long enough to be used to American ways.

The elderly, too, had changed with their new surroundings. In Russia, Jews were sometimes *tinkers*, but they could be beaten and robbed at any time. Venturing outside their own village was dangerous, and they certainly couldn't use gold fillings or sell their products aggressively. The exotic *wares*, the show of prosperity, and the loud voices all said to Isaac that America was a safe place, a place where he and his parents and his brother could prosper.

When he got a little older, Isaac was able to see that American prosperity and freedom were not without their cost. "At night, when I walk in the streets of the city," he said, "all the windows are open and I can see the life inside with all its filth and sadness. Bare, scarred tables. Countless beds, with tangled sheets and blankets. The yellow gaslight and so many, many children, and nakedness and noise."

In order to make their way in the New World, many

Immigrants wait on the upper and lower decks of a ship that is headed to Ellis Island. Many Jewish families fled persecution in Eastern Europe, settling in New York after coming to America.

immigrants, like the ones Isaac knew, lived in terrible conditions. Their apartments were tiny and often dirty; people worked too many hours a day to have any time to make things nice. Also, there were just too many people living in an apartment. A whole

Jewish immigrants to the United States often lived in crowded, filthy conditions, as this photo of a Jewish neighborhood on New York's East Side shows. The picture was taken around the year 1900. By that time, the Jewish population of the United States had increased to over 1 million, more than doubling in a ten-year period.

family would have one or two rooms to live in, and if there was extra space, they would take in a boarder. A boarder was someone, usually a young unmarried man who had just immigrated to America, who paid for meals and living space with a family.

Like many young immigrants, Isaac studied hard in American public schools and eventually moved out of the ghetto. The life of a factory worker was not for him, however. He became a writer. His books showed the world of the Jewish immigrants to all of America with compassion and sympathy, but also with a realistic attitude.

Whether it was good or bad, Isaac's life in America was always interesting to him. His new country was fast-paced, exciting, and bewildering, and sometimes it seemed to him that everything was changing at once: "The days fly by so fast that often I feel as though I were leaping over a whole generation. At times I even see myself an old man, like my grandfather, but without his confidence, without his faith."

Like other Jews who immigrated to America at the turn of the last century, Isaac had to find out how the wisdom of the old country could fit in with the rapid changes of the new one. ✸

The Touro Synagogue, built in 1763, is still standing in Newport, Rhode Island. It is the oldest Jewish house of worship in the Americas. During the early days of European settlement of North America, relatively few Jews were involved in colonization. Many of those who did come to America during the colonial period became influential in their communities.

Jews of the Colonial and Revolutionary Periods

Most of the Jews who came to America in the colonial period and in the early days of the United States were Sephardic Jews. That is, they were Jews whose national origins were in Spain or Portugal. Some of them were coming to the New World because they thought it was exciting or interesting, but most were fleeing the Inquisition. This was a special court that investigated people who did not follow the Roman Catholic religion. Jews were deemed to be *heretics*. They were persecuted for their beliefs and forced to either flee their homes or convert to Christianity.

The first Jews who came to the North American colonies arrived in 1621, but it wasn't until 1654 that a whole group of Jews came together. The 23 new arrivals who showed up in New Amsterdam, a Dutch colony, were trying to escape the Inquisition, which had spread throughout Spanish and Portuguese lands.

The governor of New Amsterdam, Peter Stuyvesant, *petitioned* Dutch authorities to *bar* Jews from coming to America. Some people have used that to claim that Stuyvesant was an *anti-Semite*. However, Stuyvesant also wanted to ban Lutherans, Baptists, Catholics, and Quakers from New Amsterdam. Stuyvesant didn't want anyone in his city who was not his own religion and nationality. Luckily for the first group of Jews in America, the Dutch authorities did not feel the same way. Those 23 immigrants formed a community in New Amsterdam that kept growing when the city changed its name to New York, and is now the second-largest Jewish community in the entire world.

Most of the Sephardic Jews who arrived during the colonial period had been merchants in Spain and Portugal, and they did not change their jobs when they moved to the New World. While many of the colonists in North America focused their energies on clearing and settling farmland, the Jews stayed mostly in the growing cities and traded important goods within the colony. Many Jews were also involved in successful import/export businesses, bringing colonists things they needed but could not find in the newborn settlements.

A large number of Christians came to North America as **indentured servants**. However, this practice was unheard of among Jews. Most Christians did not want to have Jewish servants, and most Jews could not afford servants in the early days of the colonies. The ones who could employed people who were already living in America.

Also, Jews in North America did not generally own slaves. In South America and the Caribbean islands, there were some Jewish slave owners, but the practice was so uncommon as to be astonishing if it happened in North America. And while the Jews of the colonial period were often merchants, only two of them were known to have been involved with buying or selling African slaves.

There are several ways to determine how large or important a Jewish community was in a colony, aside from records of immigrants, which are often incomplete. At the time of colonization, cemeteries

TOURO SYNAGOGUE

Newport, Rhode Island, was one of the first cities to designate a Jewish cemetery, doing so in 1677. However, it did not have a large or wealthy enough Jewish population for a synagogue for almost 100 years. Touro Synagogue in Newport was the first synagogue to be established in America, in 1763. Jews from all over the colonies sent money to support the building of this new synagogue. At that point, the Jews of Newport still felt uneasy enough about their history and the Inquisition that the synagogue was built with escape hatches and secret doors in case its Christian neighbors reversed their policy of tolerance. The white stone building has many Classical elements to its design but also draws on a tradition of Spanish synagogues, many of which have been destroyed. There are 12 columns supporting the gallery, representing the 12 tribes of Israel. Symbolic elements are also included in the candelabras and other parts of the architecture of the synagogue.

were strictly **segregated** by religion: only Anglicans could be buried in Anglican cemeteries, only Lutherans in Lutheran cemeteries, and so on. There was no **provision** for interdenominational or nonreligious cemeteries. One can note a large Jewish presence in a city by when that city had to establish a Jewish cemetery.

While we might assume that construction of a synagogue, or Jewish house of worship, is a good indicator of when Jews were truly established in a city, it took a long time for synagogues to be formed. Until that was possible, Jews met together in each other's houses for their

The Dutch colonial administrator Peter Stuyvesant attempted to keep Jews from settling in New Amsterdam, the colony that eventually became New York. Today, the Jewish community in New York is the second largest in the world.

religious services. Services required that 10 adult Jewish men be present for the service to be valid. (This number is called a *minyan*.) Often on the frontier, 10 adult Jewish men could not be found in the area, and a "frontier minyan" was five men.

Very few rabbis were willing to come to America in the colonial days, and this reluctance continued up until the American Civil War and beyond. Rabbis were the teachers and leaders of Jewish communities in Europe, and they set the tone for what the rest of the group was willing to do. In America, the first settlers had to get used to setting their own standards and looking to *lay* leaders to get things done. In early North American Jewish communities rabbis were highly respected when they could be found.

In 1740, the British government made a declaration that all Jews, Protestants, and Quakers were allowed citizenship in the British colonies once they had lived there for seven years. Many countries did not allow citizenship rights to people who did not follow the state religion, so this citizenship declaration was a step forward for Jews. However, the Inquisition had ended in 1720, so Sephardic Jews had mostly stopped emigrating from Spain by this point.

Like other colonists, Jews split on the issue of the United States' *secession* from Great Britain. Some Jews fought on each side of the

The English colonies in North America had been established as places where people could worship as they wished. After the American Revolution, President George Washington ensured that religious freedom would remain an important part of life in America.

GERSHOM MENDES SEIXAS

The first Jewish clergyman born in America was Gershom Mendes Seixas. He was the son of a Spanish-Jewish (Sephardic) father and a German-Jewish (Ashkenazi) mother. His parents sent him to New York to learn a trade, thinking that their son would become a doctor or perhaps a lawyer or a merchant. Instead, he found a group of Jewish people in need of a religious leader. They called themselves Congregation Shearith Israel. He became their *hazzan,* or cantor-minister. A cantor is the person who leads the prayer songs in a synagogue. A *hazzan* combines the function of a cantor and a more traditional minister, preaching to the people, leading them, and performing ceremonies such as marriage rites.

Seixas had to flee New York during the American Revolution when the British took over the city temporarily. He was a well-known patriot. He carried the ceremonial objects of the synagogue with him so that they would not be damaged. Seixas refused to minister to any Jews who did not support the American Revolution. He said that being an American came first to him. For a while, he stayed in Philadelphia with some other revolutionary Jews. After the war was over, he returned to his New York congregation. Seixas was one of the most influential people in American Judaism. He made sure that Jewish people in America saw that it was their country, too.

Revolutionary War, but they were not among the landowners who determined many aspects of the new country's government. The Constitution did not exclude Jews from the rights and duties of citizenship. However, in some states it took until 1840 for Jews to have voting rights and the ability to hold public offices.

George Washington became the first head of state to guarantee religious freedom to Jews forever, in 1790. He also promised them full citizenship throughout the land. For a group of people that had been treated poorly and kicked out of many European countries, this was a welcome step forward. The New World looked even more like a land of opportunity—and different groups of European Jews started to notice. ✺

Two Jewish Americans talk in a deli in Brooklyn. Many of the Jews who came to the United States and Canada during the early decades of the 19th century were from the region now known as Germany.

3 The German Jews

In the early and middle 1800s, the Jews who came to the United States and Canada were mostly Ashkenazi Jews. Ashkenazi is a term that covers all Northern and Eastern European Jews. However, most of the Ashkenazi Jews who came to America in this time period were from Germany. In Germany Jews were forced to live in cramped ghettos, and the government passed many regulations limiting their ability to do business and lead normal lives. Many fled to America for greater freedom.

Some European Jews thought that they wouldn't have to come to America to be free. In France during the early 19th century Napoleon established a legal system that allowed Jews many personal freedoms. However, Napoleon's government was eventually overthrown, and Jews were returned to their previous oppressed states. Many grew discouraged with life in Europe and fled to America to have their rights as human beings protected.

Meanwhile, the established Jewish community took a hard hit during the War of 1812, when exports from the United States went from $61 million a year to $7 million a year. They had to regroup and change their businesses to survive. Many Jews went into government service. Others opened general stores, which later became retail stores; became **peddlers**; or went into the fur trade.

After the Louisiana Purchase, the German Jews came to America in full force. They spread further west than most of the Sephardic Jews had. Many of them became peddlers as well. They would travel around the developing countryside with necessary goods that the farmers could not produce for themselves—things like sewing needles and pots and pans.

Every so often, they would return to their new home city to replenish their stock of trade goods. St. Louis, Milwaukee, Cleveland, and Albany were popular choices for home cities for these peddlers because they were close to lakes and rivers, so that shipping was easy. Some Jewish men left wives and children in their home cities. Many were bachelors who had come to America by themselves. Some of the bachelors married Christian girls. During this time, many Jews who married Christians converted to Christianity.

On the road, peddlers would sometimes run into Jewish clergymen. The most common people who traveled were *maggids*, Jewish **itinerant** preachers. Maggids would ride throughout a particular area, ministering to different small Jewish communities. These communities were too small to support a rabbi, or even a congregation, by themselves, but they could give a *maggid* food and a place to stay, and perhaps a few pennies if they had any to spare. **Meshulahs** also traveled around the country. These were people who collected for Jewish char- ities. With the help of meshulahs, Jewish people who lived on the frontier could still help other Jewish people back in the cities of the East and around the world.

A gold pointer is used to help a reader follow the lines of Hebrew text in this copy of the Torah, the book containing Jewish teachings and laws. In Europe during the first half of 19th century, some Jews set out to change their religion. They argued that because the Jews were no longer a nation, but were citizens of many nations, they no longer had to follow all the restrictions of the Jewish law. Although Reform Judaism, as it was called, never had any great success in Europe, by 1880 most of the synagogues in the United States had become reform. Most also became members of the Union of American Hebrew Congregations, which was formed in 1873.

YEHUDISHKEIT

From the earliest days of colonization, American Jews were concerned about acting Jewish enough. The word *Yehudishkeit*, meaning "Jewishness," was used often in letters to relatives in Europe. They wanted to make sure that their traditions and their religion were not lost in a new world that had so few Jews in it. In Europe, there were more laws restricting Jewish behavior, but it was also recognized that Jews kept a different Sabbath day from Christians and had different dietary practices. With so few Jews, it was hard to get a community together to practice the faith. Also, people who had lived for a long time without following traditional Jewish practices were more likely to abandon them completely.

Women immigrants were particularly disturbed by the problem of trying to raise their children in a neighborhood with no *Yehudishkeit*. One early American, Rebecca Samuel, wrote to her parents, "Dear parents, Jewishness is pushed aside here. There are here [in Petersburg, Virginia] 10 or 12 Jews, and they are not worthy of being called Jews." She writes about the food and clothing practices that were ignored. Rebecca was also upset by Jews who kept their stores open on the Sabbath—a common practice in America.

Many Jewish people who were concerned about *Yehudishkeit* made an effort to move to more Jewish areas. Rebecca wrote, "You must believe me that in our house we all live as Jews as much as we can....My children cannot learn anything here, nothing Jewish, nothing of general culture." She ends by telling her parents that they are moving to Charleston, a city with several hundred Jews. In larger communities, it was easier to become American and still keep what was important about being Jewish.

By 1850 there were more than 50,000 Jews in North America, and the numbers were rising fast. However, when the Civil War broke out, immigration to the United States almost completely stopped. No one wanted to come to a country that was at war with itself. Even crowded ghettos and prejudiced governments looked better than that.

One of the biggest cases of anti-Semitism in American history was the expulsion of Jews from Tennessee. General Ulysses S. Grant was concerned about everyone who was trying to get in and make money from the people of Tennessee during the war. These people were called speculators, and in addition to taking advantage of people, they tended to break laws and cause trouble. Grant decided that the real problem was with Jewish speculators, so he issued an order that every Jew had to leave Tennessee in December 1862. President Lincoln, however, realized that the Jews were not the only speculators who were at fault. He overturned Grant's order and let Jewish people back into Tennessee as soon as he heard what had happened.

While America was going through its Civil War, there was a rift in Judaism around the world as well. Some Jews in Germany were concerned about how much Jewish life focused on rituals. They didn't think that religious practices, like eating **kosher** foods and wearing certain clothes, were important to being Jewish. They also thought that men and women should sit together during worship services, and that women should have a voice in their congregations. These new Jews called themselves Reform Jews.

Eventually, the more traditional Jews formed into two **sects**: the

Orthodox Jews, who were the most traditional; and the Conservative Jews, who tried to strike a balance between the traditions of the Orthodox Jews and the new ideas of the Reform Jews. All three Jewish traditions are well represented in modern America, but in the 1800s, most Jews were already acting more like the Reform branch. There weren't as many rabbis available as there had been in Europe, so they had to make due with less formal religious ceremonies. Then, when more American rabbis received training, they adapted themselves to the way of life their congregations had established. As more traditional rabbis came to America later on, the Orthodox and Conservative movements gained strength.

In this photograph from the 1950s, cars drive past a Sears store in Los Angeles. A Jewish American named Richard Warren Sears founded the department store chain as a mail-order business in Minneapolis during the early 1890s. By 1903, the company had annual sales of more than $11 million. Today Sears is one of the largest companies in the United States.

After the Civil War, Jews tried to get back to their normal lives, just like the rest of the country. Some peddlers made enough money to establish permanent retail businesses for themselves. General stores grew into department stores, which grew into chain department stores. Jewish Americans were responsible for the founding or major growth of Bloomingdale's, Filene's, Neiman Marcus, Sears, and other large chain stores.

As German-Jewish people became more successful in America, they started to face more **prejudice** from other Americans. People who felt fine about shopping in stores owned by Jews didn't want to have Jews in their country clubs or fraternities. Some private schools, hotels, and neighborhoods also began to implement rules that kept Jews out.

In most of America, this prejudice did not become violent. But there were parts of the Deep South where people felt so strongly about not having Jews around that they looted and burned their Jewish neighbors' houses and stores.

ISAAC LEESER

In Europe, it was hard for Jews to get their religious works widely published. As soon as American Jews were well established, some of them started publishing houses, printing books and newspapers for the Jewish immigrant community. Some Jewish publishing houses exported their materials to European countries as well.

One of the more prominent Jewish publishers in America was Isaac Leeser, who came over from Germany when he was 18. He helped the prominent Seixas family in their religious school and wrote stirring defenses of Jews for the local newspaper. After he became a hazzan in Philadelphia, Leeser decided to put out books about being a Jew. His first effort, *Instruction in Mosaic Religion* was well received. Over the course of his career, he translated the Bible and several Sephardic prayer books into English. He also wrote textbooks and sermons about Judaism.

Leeser was one of the first Jews to try to get Jewish Americans to feel like a community. One of his biggest accomplishments was to found *The Occident and American Jewish Advocate*, a large Jewish newspaper. It lasted for more than 25 years in its original form and covered a wide range of news and opinion items.

The Influx from Eastern Europe

Towards the late 1800s, Ashkenazi Jews still comprised most of the Jewish immigrants to the United States. However, they were no longer coming from Germany in such large numbers. Instead, Jews from Russia, Poland, the Ukraine, and other eastern European countries were pouring into the country at the turn of the last century.

There was a good reason why they were leaving eastern Europe. Alexander III, the Russian *czar*, had decided he wanted to get rid of all the Jews in the Russian territories. He and one of his advisors, Konstantin Pobedonostsev, stated that they wanted the Jews to have disappeared by "one-third conversion, one-third emigration, and one-third starvation."

Jewish immigrants wave as their ship passes the Statue of Liberty in New York harbor. This colored postcard was made from a photograph taken in 1892. During the second half of the 19th century, the number of Jewish Americans increased from about 50,000 to nearly 1.1 million.

Jews in Russia already had to live inside the Pale of Settlement, a region specifically created for them. Jews caught outside the Pale were not protected by the law and could be prosecuted for leaving. Inside the Pale, Jewish villages often existed side by side with their more prosperous Christian counterparts. Up until 1882, however,

The harsh policies of the Russian czar Alexander III led to violent pogroms in which thousands of Jews were killed. Many others left Russia and the other countries of eastern Europe for the United States and Canada.

persecution of Jews was an issue specific to each village. After 1882, pogroms and expulsions became part of Russian law.

A pogrom was a systematic campaign of intimidation, destruction, and violence aimed at Jews. In pogroms, Jewish homes and businesses were looted and burned, and Jewish people were beaten, raped, and killed. The Russian government approved of the pogrom system, and government officials and soldiers often participated in these horrific events.

In the 10 years after 1882, the number of Russian and eastern European Jews who immigrated to America was so large that there were almost four times as many Jews in North America at the end of 1892 as there had been at the end of 1882. And they continued to come. Three-quarters of the Jews in the whole world had lived in Russia and eastern Europe at the beginning of the 1880s. They were all persecuted, and most wanted to leave. The United States and Canada were the most welcoming countries for them. In 40 years, the North American Jewish population increased by sixteen times.

In 1903, the Russian czar's government noticed that it was getting less and less stable. In response, it became more violent. Pogroms increased. Violence against Christian-Russian laborers also increased. When this happened, the Russian Jews sometimes became *scapegoats* for their neighbors' frustrations. It was even more dangerous to be a Jew in Russia from 1903 to 1906, and the immigration numbers reflected it.

However, it was hard to come to America. A steamship ticket for one person cost $34 in 1903. Most people earned $5 a week when they came to America, and that was more than they had earned in their home countries. In order to raise $34 for each member of the family, families sold literally everything they owned. They arrived in America with only the clothes on their backs, totally broke.

Furthermore, arriving at Ellis Island did not mean that they had safely immigrated to America. Doctors examined immigrants closely to see if they had signs of any major contagious diseases. Tuberculosis in particular had the stigma of being a "Jewish disease," even though Jews did not have it all that often. Each year, immigration officials turned away 1 to 2.5 percent of the people who were attempting to come to America.

Many Americans felt that the country should remain populated mostly by Protestants of British or Northern European descent. Jews were seen as outsiders, not able to become "real" Americans. Jews who were not from western Europe were considered to be even more foreign and strange, and presented more of a threat to some people's concept of America.

Strangely enough, some American Jews actually shared this view. They had become thoroughly Americanized and feared that the newcomers would make Christians think Jews spoke poor English, dressed strangely, and had odd customs. Many more eastern European Jews followed Orthodox practices, in contrast to the large American-Reform Jewish community. Also, most charities were run by religious organizations, so the established Jewish Americans were afraid they'd be overrun by *destitute* newcomers needing lots of help.

As it turned out, many of the newcomers wanted to be Americanized as quickly as possible. They chose to wear American clothes as soon as

A group of Orthodox Jews prays together. As more emigrants from eastern Europe arrived in America, they established communities in large cities in the United States and Canada.

they could afford them and joined American Reform synagogues. Others held on to their old ways, however, changing more gradually to American customs. Still others brought small sects of Judaism with them. The most prominent among these were the Hasidim, a strictly Orthodox sect that focused on mysticism. Even today, the Hasidic community resists assimilation into mainstream American culture.

This colored postcard, made from a photograph by Jacob Riis, shows a pantmaker's workshop on New York City's Lower East Side. The entire family pictured here worked morning to night to make $8 a week. Many Jewish immigrants worked in New York's garment industry.

Most Jewish immigrants arrived in the North Atlantic states, with New York's Ellis Island handling a vast majority of the newcomers. Most Jews settled in big cities like New York, Toronto, Chicago, and Los Angeles. In these cities, Jewish groups started settlement houses. A settlement house was a place where new immigrants could stay while they got on their feet. The workers at a settlement house helped newcomers to find honest jobs and work their way out of poverty so that they didn't have to turn to crime to feed themselves. Many German-Jewish Americans who had been born here tried to teach classes to the "***greenhorn***" newcomers in English, manners, and behaving like Americans.

A group of Jews called assimilationists thought that the recent immigrants should be sent to cities all across America, so that everyone would have a few Jews in their town. They thought this would make people less likely to be prejudiced against Jews. However, assimilationism didn't work all that well. Jewish communities emerged in most medium-sized cities, but not in small towns.

Since an overwhelming majority of Jewish immigrants spoke little or no English, they had to find jobs with other people who spoke Yiddish. The garment industry was a common starting place. Men, women, and children would work together in ***sweatshops***. Their bosses would pick up loads of pre-cut pieces to be stitched together into clothing. The workers would have to pay for their own sewing machines to do the work. If they didn't have a sewing machine, the bosses took part of their pay each week until the sewing machine was paid for. The work was hard and dirty, and the working conditions were often terrible. However, it was a large improvement to the immigrants. The freedoms of America and the chance to make their lives better made the hardships worthwhile. Only five percent of Jewish immigrants returned to their home countries, as opposed to one-third of non-Jews who came to North America.

When they could get enough money and their English had improved, some Jewish immigrants bought pushcarts. They walked through the streets of the cities, calling out to people to buy their fruit, ice cream, or any of a number of other products. The more ambitious started small stores. A full quarter of the Jewish people who were the breadwinners for their households were self-employed.

These occupations put food on the table, but Jewish-American parents wanted something more for their children. Some of them focused on education as a road out of the Jewish ghetto and into a middle-class life. Even children who were indifferent to schooling were urged to study hard so that they could someday become wealthy doctors or lawyers and support their old parents.

In Europe, most Jewish children went to Jewish religious schools called *heder*. Education had always been valued in Jewish culture. However, in America, most Jewish children went to public schools. It wasn't until large numbers of Jews were wealthy that *heder* could be started in America. By that time, Jewish Americans were used to sending their children to public schools. Also, most Jewish youngsters went to colleges instead of Jewish *yeshivas* (religious schools of higher learning). A few *yeshivas* were established, mostly to train rabbis, but the **secular** college system was usually where bright young Jews got their degrees.

JACOB SCHIFF

Of all the 19th-century Jews who were committed to helping the Jewish community, Jacob Schiff was probably the most successful. He was related to almost every wealthy Jewish family in America. Schiff managed to organize some assimilationists into finding homes in the West for new Jewish immigrants, raising over $50,000 towards this purpose. He also remained active in business, banking, and politics.

Schiff stood up for Russian-born Jews who had gotten American citizenship when many Sephardic and German Jewish Americans did not want them around. He also raised money to send to European Jewish communities to help poor people come to America. Schiff convinced some Christians to reach out with him to the oppressed Jews of Eastern Europe. Without his help, many would not have escaped to America.

Other Jewish Americans wanted something better for themselves right away. They didn't want to wait for their children to join the middle class. Labor unions looked like the way to get the money they deserved for the difficult jobs they were doing. They organized strikes and picketed factories that had unfair practices. Sometimes wealthier Jewish ladies would join their poorer sisters in boycotting stores or products with unfair practices.

Large percentages of Jews were drawn through labor unions to the Socialist Party. They supported the Socialist party for many years, until Franklin Delano Roosevelt made an effort to reach out to Jewish labor leaders in his campaign for the presidency. Jewish-American voters

Writer/director Mel Brooks receives a Tony Award for the stage version of *The Producers*. The Broadway smash hit was based on a film he had written and directed more than 30 years earlier. Brooks has been a very successful director, which such comedy films to his credit as *Blazing Saddles, Young Frankenstein, Spaceballs,* and *Robin Hood: Men in Tights.*

THE YIDDISH THEATER

One of the favorite pastimes of Jewish immigrants was the Yiddish theater. Jewish people from all walks of life attended these plays. Families sat next to bachelors; rabbis shared benches with socialist and anarchist agitators. Sometimes, the Yiddish theatre was the only thing Jewish people could agree upon.

Some plays were Yiddish translations of English-language classics. *Hamlet* and *King Lear* were particularly popular. Others were original plays written in Yiddish. Popular themes were historical Jewish triumphs and victories, as in *Shulamit* and *Bar Kochba*. But the Yiddish theatre also turned a mirror on the community, satirizing and sympathizing with the plight of the newcomers to America.

As more Jews spoke English at home rather than Yiddish, the Yiddish theaters died out, but Jewish actors continued to shine. Major Jewish actors, directors, and comics have included Mel Brooks, Zero Mostel, Madeline Kahn, Billy Crystal, Steven Spielberg, Woody Allen, George Burns, Gracie Allen, and many others. Most Hollywood studios were founded by Jewish Americans—including Paramount, MGM, Columbia, Warner Brothers, and Universal.

who had been voting Socialist switched to the Democratic Party almost unanimously. While no political party represents an entire ethnic group, many Jewish Americans have continued to give the Democratic Party their political support to this day.

Jewish men and women also served as labor leaders. Some of them made major efforts to bridge the big gap between workers. One of the largest obstacles to labor unions was the fact that ethnic groups didn't share common languages. Some Jewish labor leaders, such as Abraham Cahan, tried to communicate with members of other ethnic groups, using sign language when other means were impossible. Jews such as Samuel Gompers made their voices heard in the larger labor unions.

Sometimes labor unions were divided up by ethnic group. The Jews had their own labor unions, such as the United Hebrew Trades and the Jewish Workers Educational Society. Interestingly enough, people who were involved in labor unions were much less likely to be involved in synagogue life. For some, Judaism ceased to be a religion. They saw it only as an ethnic group or way of life. Those who were interested in Karl Marx and Socialism often disliked the rabbis, resenting their influence on the community in religious and financial matters.

During the early 20th century, the role of women was changing in all of America, and that was also true in the Jewish community. Upper-class Jewish women still were mostly housewives and mothers, but the lower classes could not afford not to have some income from the wife of the family. Married women sometimes took in sewing work that they could do in their homes. They also helped with businesses, if their husbands became small business owners. One of the most common ways a wife made money for her family was to take in boarders.

At this time, most Jewish immigrant girls worked in the sweatshops until they could get married. The most common occupation was that of a seamstress, sewing shirts or dresses or pants for the garment trade.

Jewish-American girls whose families had lived in America for a generation or more usually spoke better English. Because of this, they could often get better jobs as librarians, teachers, and office workers. However, even these jobs did not pay very much.

Sometimes women became active in the labor movements to try to make things better for themselves and their families. Most labor movements were only sympathetic to women's rights up to a point, however. They often focused on men who were earning a living to support their families. The equal two-income household was not yet a reality in the Jewish community or elsewhere in America.

At the beginning of the 1920s, many Americans were concerned about immigration. They wanted America to stay more or less as it had been when they were growing up, with the same proportions of ethnic groups. To try to keep the face of America the same, Congress passed the Johnson Act in 1921. The Johnson Act was a bill that limited the number of immigrants from any ethnic group who could come to America in a given year. That number was proportional to how many Americans of that ethnic group had already lived here back in 1890. Since most of the Jewish people in America had come after 1890, their immigration was cut back severely.

By the time the Johnson Act passed, the Communist government had already overthrown the Russian tsar. Some prominent Communists were Jews, so pogroms were no longer aimed at Jewish people. Some thought there was no longer much of a reason to leave Eastern Europe. The events of the next 20 years would prove them sadly mistaken. ✺

A woman views photographs of Holocaust victims at the Museum of Jewish Heritage, which opened in New York in 1997. Nearly 6 million German and eastern European Jews were killed on the orders of Nazi dictator Adolf Hitler.

5 The Holocaust and Beyond

When Adolf Hitler came to power in Germany in 1933, he talked often about how much he hated Jews and how Jews were a problem that required a drastic solution. Some Americans didn't think he really meant that he would have Jews killed, but it was clear that life in Germany was not going to be pleasant for Jewish people. In the years before World War II, the Johnson Act was waived to allow 157,000 German Jewish refugees to immigrate to the United States.

Sadly, this number was only a small fraction of the number of Jews who would be killed in Hitler's concentration camps between 1937 and 1945. Some people chose not to leave Germany; they, too, did not believe that Hitler was really going to kill them. Eventually, war broke out, and it was illegal to leave. Some Jewish people were smuggled out of Germany and the territories occupied by it. However, it was much harder to get to America in wartime conditions, and many of them stayed in countries like England and Sweden until the war was over.

One of the major problems during the war years in getting to America was transportation. That was not the only obstacle, however. From 1940 on, many *visas* for German Jews to enter the United States went unused. Breckinridge Long, the official in charge of determining whether visas applied to specific people, decided to be restrictive. Like many Americans, he didn't believe that things in Germany were as bad as he had heard. He didn't want too many Jews in America. So even when some Americans tried to help German Jews, others made it hard for them to arrive here.

Finally, in 1943, a man named Henry Morgenthau went to President Roosevelt about the situation. Morgenthau was the Secretary of the Treasury. He was the highest-ranked Jewish American in Roosevelt's Cabinet. Morgenthau convinced Roosevelt to establish the War Refugee Board in 1944.

The War Refugee Board focused on getting the Jews out of Hungary, since that was the only country that had a large number of Jews left alive. The United States government also provided "temporary housing" for some refugees in places like Oswego, New York. In both cases, some non-Jews were included for political purposes. It was easier to get politicians to agree to funding for housing and immigration if these things helped all refugees, not just the Jewish ones.

Approximately six million Jews died in the Holocaust. At the beginning of the Holocaust, North America was home to less than a third of the Jews in the world. After the Holocaust, nearly half of the Jews in the world lived on this one continent. Jews and Gentiles (non-Jews) alike believe that it is important to remember the Holocaust so that nothing like it can ever happen again.

After World War II ended, Congress again waived the Johnson Act so that refugees from war-torn Europe could find a place to rebuild their lives. Many Jewish people were included in the 192,000 refugees who took advantage of this opportunity from 1944 to 1959.

Henry Morganthau (right) speaks with President Franklin D. Roosevelt in 1935. Morganthau, a Jewish American member of Roosevelt's cabinet, persuaded the president to establish a War Refugee Board in 1944 to help European Jews escape persecution during World War II. However, by this time it was too late for millions of German and eastern European Jews.

These emaciated survivors of the concentration camp
at Ebensee, Austria, were freed by the U.S. Army in
May 1945. After the war, some of the European Jews
who had survived Hitler's Third Reich came to
America. Others moved to Palestine, where the state
of Israel would be formed in 1948.

During the years after World War II, the United States and other countries helped Zionist Jews found the nation of Israel. A Zionist was someone who believed that Palestine, in the Middle East, had always been the Jewish homeland and that Jews needed a country of their own to call home. Some American Jews enthusiastically supported Israel and even wanted to move there. Others felt that they were better off remaining in the United States or Canada. Some did not have to choose. To this day, Israel is the only country where an American can have dual citizenship that is recognized by the United States government.

In the years since Israel was founded, the United States has provided support for its government. America has helped Israel in times of war and peace. Cross-immigration continues from the U.S. to Israel and back. By the year 2000, an estimated 300,000 American citizens were Jews who had emigrated from Israel.

The political situation in the Middle East has never been stable, and from 1960 to 1970, Congress waived the Johnson Act one last time to let Jews from various countries in the Arabic Middle East **emigrate**. Jews also came from Cuba, which was the focus of many conflicts in that era. Between the two regions, 73,000 Jews fled to America in that decade.

One of the other major developments of the 1960s was the increase in interfaith marriage. In 1960, less than 10 percent of all Jewish Americans married Gentiles. By 1970, a third did. Now, half of all Jewish Americans marry Gentiles. However, 28 percent of the Gentiles who marry Jewish Americans now convert to Judaism.

From the 1970s to the 1990s, the focus of immigration switched from the Middle East and Cuba to the former Soviet Union. Those Jews who had remained in the Soviet Union were being allowed to leave in unprecedented numbers. One hundred thousand of them arrived in the United States during those two decades. However, it was a small trickle compared to the flood from their Russian cousins at the turn of the previous century.

Jewish Americans still practice their unique religious and cultural habits in various ways. However, the days when they lived in neighbor-

Film director Steven Spielberg has scored some of the biggest box-office hits of all time, including *Jaws, ET: The Extra-Terrestrial, Raiders of the Lost Ark,* and *Saving Private Ryan.* In 1993 he brought to the screen a film that he admitted was important to him personally: *Schindler's List,* the story of a factory owner who saved the lives of more than 1,000 Polish Jews during World War II. The film won seven Oscars, including Best Picture and Best Director.

Moroccan Jews converse at the Western Wall in Jerusalem. Jewish Americans contributed money and support to help build Israel. Today, the United States is one of Israel's closest allies.

hoods apart from non-Jews are gone. Jewish Americans work in every profession in this country. They have achieved a very difficult feat: assimilation without the loss of their identity.

No one knows if Jewish immigration to the United States will continue at significant rates. It is clear, however, that Jewish Americans have changed over the course of history—and that they have changed the course of American history themselves. ✹

Important Jewish Immigrants and Jewish Americans

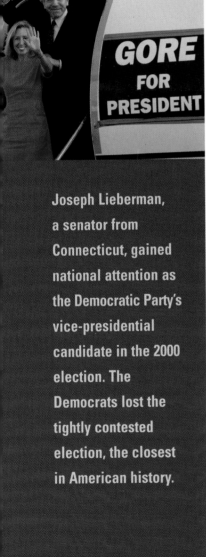

Joseph Lieberman, a senator from Connecticut, gained national attention as the Democratic Party's vice-presidential candidate in the 2000 election. The Democrats lost the tightly contested election, the closest in American history.

Isaac Asimov, science fiction writer

Judah Benjamin, Confederate statesman

Irving Berlin, composer

Louis Brandeis, judge and writer

Bob Dylan, musician

Albert Einstein, physicist

Michael Eisner, entertainment executive

Betty Freidan, feminist

George and Ira Gershwin, composers

Samuel Goldwyn, co-founder of the movie studio MGM

Samuel Gompers, labor leader

Ann Landers and Abigail Van Buren, advice columnists

Emma Lazarus, poet

Norman Lear, director

Louis Mayer, co-founder of MGM

Golda Meir, prime minister of Israel

Steven Spielberg, director

Gloria Steinem, feminist

Barbra Streisand, musician and actress

Edward Teller, physicist

Al Yankovic, musician

Immigration Figures

Year	Jewish Population	% of U.S. Population	% of Jews in the world
1790	1,350	.03	
1800	1,600	.03	.06
1810	2,000	.03	
1820	2,700	.03	
1830	4,500	.03	
1840	15,000	.09	
1850	50,000	.22	1.05
1860	150,000	.48	
1870	200,000	.52	
1880	250,000	.5	3.27
1890	450,000	.71	
1900	1,050,000	1.38	9.91
1910	2,043,000	2.22	15.91
1920	3,600,000	3.41	22.86
1930	4,400,000	3.58	29.23
1940	4,700,000	3.65	30.46
1950	5,000,000	3.32	43.48
1960	5,400,000	3	42.97
1970	5,691,000	2.8	40.94
1980	5,900,000	2.42	40.75
1990	5,800,000	2.3	45.00
2000	6,061,000	2.2	46.64

(U.S. Census figures)

Glossary

Anti-Semitism prejudice against Jewish people.

Bar to keep out or exclude.

Czar the emperor of Russia before the Russian Revolution in 1917; also spelled tsar.

Destitute lacking possessions and resources.

Emigrate to leave one's country of origin to live elsewhere.

Ghetto an area of a city in which Jews were forced to live.

Greenhorn a newcomer to America; a recent immigrant.

Heretic a dissenter from established church dogma.

Indentured servant a person who signs and is bound by a contract to work for another for a specified time in return for payment of travel expenses.

Itinerant traveling from place to place.

Kosher food that Jewish people are allowed to eat, according to ancient laws in the Torah. Kosher food must be specially prepared.

Lay not religious.

Meshulah a representative of a Jewish charity who traveled the countryside looking for donations; also called *shohets*.

Peddler one who sells merchandise on the street or from door to door.

Persecute to harass someone because of his or her beliefs.

Petition to make a formal, written request.

Prejudice an attitude of hostility directed against an individual, a group, a race, or their supposed characteristics.

Provision a measure taken beforehand to deal with a possible need.

Scapegoat one who bears the blame for others.

Secession formal withdrawal from an organization.

Sect a group adhering to a distinctive doctrine or to a leader.

Secular not religious.

Segregate to separate from the general society.

Steerage a section of accommodations in a ship for the lowest-paying passengers.

Sweatshop a shop or factory in which workers are employed for long hours at low wages and under unhealthy conditions.

Tinker a roaming worker who mends utensils.

Virility masculinity.

Visa a stamp on a passport indicating that someone has permission to enter a country.

Wares manufactured articles, products of art or craft, or farm produce.

Further Reading

Dimont, Max. *The Jews in America.* New York: Simon and Schuster, 1978.

Howe, Irving, and Kenneth Libo. *How We Lived: A Documentary History of Immigrant Jews in America, 1880–1930.* New York: Richard Marek Publishers, 1979.

Karp, Abraham. *A History of the Jews in America.* Northvale: Jason Aronson, Inc., 1997.

Morais, Vamberto. *A Short History of Anti-Semitism.* New York: Norton and Company, Inc., 1976.

Sorin, Gerald. *Tradition Transformed: The Jewish Experience in North America.* Baltimore: Johns Hopkins University Press, 1997.

Finding your Jewish-American ancestors

Carmack, Sharon DeBartolo. *A Geneaologist's Guide to Discovering Your Immigrant and Ethnic Ancestors.* Cincinnati: Betterway Books, 2000.

Guzik, Estelle, ed. *Genealogical Resources in the New York Metropolitan Area.* New York: Jewish Genealogical Society, 2000.

Kurzweil, Arthur. *From Generation to Generation: How to Trace Your Jewish Genealogy and Personal History.* New York: HarperCollins, 1994.

Press, D. *Jewish Americans.* North Bellmore, N.Y.: Benchmark Books, 1995.

Zubatsky, David S., and Irwin M. Berent. *Sourcebook for Jewish Genealogy and Family Histories.* 2 vols. Teaneck, N.J.: Avotaynu, 1996.

Internet Resources

http://www.census.gov

The official website of the U.S. Bureau of the Census contains information about the most recent census taken in 2000.

http://www.statcan.ca/start.html

The website for Canada's Bureau of Statistics, which includes population information updated for the most recent census in July 2001.

http://www.balchinstitute.org

This Web site is dedicated to documenting information about the experience of immigrants to the United States.

http://shamash.org/places/boston/synagog/vilna/timeline.html

A timeline of Jewish immigration to the United States

http://www.jewishmuseum.net/American.htm

This website provides a historical overview of Jewish immigration.

http://www.nhc.rtp.nc.us:8080/tserve/nineteen/nkeyinfo/judaism.htm

Jewish immigration during the 19th century is the subject of this website.

Index

African, 18
Albany, 26
Alexander III, czar of Russia, 35
Anglicans, 18–19
Anti-Semitism, 17, 29
Ashkenazi Jews, 25, 35

Baptists, 17
Bloomingdale's, 31
Bonaparte, Napoleon, 25
Brazil, 17

Cahan, Abraham, 46
Canada, 25, 37, 53
Caribbean, 18
Chicago, 41
Christianity, 11, 17, 18, 26, 35, 37, 38
Civil War, 21, 29, 31
Cleveland, 26
Communist, 47
Conservative Jews, 29
Cuba, 53–54

Democratic Party, 45
Dutch, 17

Ellis Island, 11, 38, 41

Filene's, 31

Germany, 11, 25–26, 29, 32, 35, 41, 49–50
Gompers, Samuel, 46
Grant, Ulysses S., 29
Great Britain, 21, 38, 49

Hasidic Jews, 39
Hitler, Adolf, 49
Holocaust, 50
Hungary, 50

Inquisition, 17, 21

Israel, 53

Jewish, 11–15, 17, 18, 21, 25–32,
    35–47, 49–55
Jewish Workers Educational Society, 46
Johnson Act, 47, 49–50, 53

Lincoln, Abraham, 29
Long, Breckinridge, 49
Los Angeles, 41
Louisiana Purchase, 26
Lower East Side, 12
Lutherans, 17, 19

Marx, Karl, 46
Middle East, 53–54
Milwaukee, 26
Morgenthau, Henry, 50

Neiman Marcus, 31
New Amsterdam, 17
New York, 11, 12, 18, 41

Orthodox Jews, 29, 38, 39
Oswego, New York, 50

Pale of Settlement, 35
Pobedonostsev, Konstantin, 35
Poland, 35
Portugal, 17, 18
Protestants, 21, 38

Quakers, 17, 21

Raboy, Isaac, 11–15
Reform Jews, 29, 38–39
Revolutionary War, 21
Roman Catholic Church, 17
Roosevelt, Franklin Delano, 43, 50
Russia, 11, 12, 35–37, 54

Photo Credits

Contributors

Barry Moreno has been librarian and historian at the Ellis Island Immigration Museum and the Statue of Liberty National Monument since 1988. He is the author of *The Statue of Liberty Encyclopedia*, which was published by Simon & Schuster in October 2000. He is a native of Los Angeles, California. After graduation from California State University at Los Angeles, where he earned a degree in history, he joined the National Park Service as a seasonal park ranger at the Statue of Liberty; he eventually became the monument's librarian. In his spare time, Barry enjoys reading, writing, and studying foreign languages and grammar. His biography has been included in *Who's Who Among Hispanic Americans*, *The Directory of National Park Service Historians*, *Who's Who in America*, and *The Directory of American Scholars*.

Marissa Lingen is a freelance writer of fiction and educational materials. She was the 1999 winner of the Asimov Award. She is married and lives in Hayward, California.